SPOTLIGHT
THE RUSSIAN REVOLUTION

HEREFORD AND WORCESTER
COUNTY LIBRARIES
6 505821
J 947.0841

KIDDERMINSTER

Michael Gibson

0850787548482 1

SPOTLIGHT ON HISTORY

Spotlight on the Age of Exploration and Discovery
Spotlight on the Age of Revolution
Spotlight on the Agricultural Revolution
Spotlight on the Cold War
Spotlight on the Collapse of Empires
Spotlight on Elizabethan England
Spotlight on the English Civil War
Spotlight on the First World War
Spotlight on the Industrial Revolution
Spotlight on Industry in the Twentieth Century
Spotlight on Medieval Europe
Spotlight on Post-War Europe
Spotlight on the Reformation
Spotlight on Renaissance Europe
Spotlight on the Rise of Modern China
Spotlight on the Russian Revolution
Spotlight on the Second World War
Spotlight on the Victorians

Cover Illustration: 'On the ruins of capitalism towards worldwide brotherhood of the workers', by Nikolai Kocherghin 1920

First published in 1986 by Wayland (Publishers) Ltd
61 Western Road, Hove, East Sussex, BN3 1JD, England

© Copyright 1986 Wayland (Publishers) Ltd

British Library Cataloguing in Publication Data
Gibson, Michael, 1936
Spotlight on the Russian Revolution (Spotlight on history)
1. Soviet Union—Politics and government—20th century
    I. Title   II. Series
    947.08   DK 246

ISBN 0-85078-754-8

Typeset, printed and bound in the UK by The Bath Press, Avon

CONTENTS

1	Origins	4
2	What is to be Done?	11
3	Growing Pains	19
4	End of an Era	28
5	The November Revolution	38
6	All Power to the Soviets	45
7	An Era of Transition	51
8	Stalin's Revolution	58
9	The Unfinished Revolution	64
	Date Chart	71
	Glossary	72
	Further Reading	74
	Index	75

1 ORIGINS

Although Russia is part of Europe, it has developed in isolation. When the Roman legions were conquering the West and spreading the culture which is still the basis of Western European life, Russia was a land of wild Slav tribes. The influence of Graeco-Roman culture did not reach Russia until the tenth century, when it was converted to Christianity by Greek Orthodox monks. Thanks to their success, some Russians have always regarded Constantinople, now called Istanbul, as the centre of civilization. This belief has continued until the present day.

The original 'Rus' were Vikings who set up trading posts along the banks of the great Russian rivers. As the trade between Scandinavia and the Mediterranean world prospered, important city-states developed at Novgorod, Pskov and Kiev. While the feudal system of warrior landlords and serf labourers developed in Western Europe, the Russians continued their separate existence.

Christianity was introduced into Russia in the tenth century by Greek Orthodox monks.

The Mongol conquerors of Russia were extremely ruthless. This manuscript illustration depicts invading Mongol troops crossing over a frozen river.

Mongol dominance

In the thirteenth century, the Russians became still more isolated from other Europeans by the Mongol Conquest. The 'Golden Horde' seized control of Russia and dominated it for three hundred years. The Mongols' methods were extremely brutal. A visitor to Kiev in 1246 reported: 'We found an innumerable multitude of dead men's skulls and bones lying upon the earth. For it was a very large and populous city, but it was now ... brought to nothing; for there do scarce remain two hundred houses, the inhabitants whereof are kept in extreme bondage.' Some historians believe that Russian respect for autocracy—the unchallenged rule of a single leader—arose out of this period of deference to their Mongol overlords.

Ivan the Terrible began his blood stained career at the age of fourteen, putting a Royal Council to death. His cruelty increased with his age and finally he murdered his own son.

Ivan the Terrible
When the Mongol Empire started to crumble, during the later Middle Ages, the Russians established small but vigorous Grand Duchies. Moscow was the most successful, thanks to a series of efficient and ambitious rulers. Ivan the Terrible (1530–84), Moscow's most famous ruler, ruthlessly eliminated his rivals. In Novgorod, for instance, he 'ransacked, robbed and spoiled all that were herein of their jewels, plate and treasure; murdered the people, young and old, burnt all their household stuff, merchandises and warehouses.' As soon as he had subjugated the Slavs, he attacked the Mongols and captured their capitals of Kazan and Astrakhan. Ivan called himself Tsar or Emperor and Autocrat of all the Russians. He modelled himself on the Byzantine rulers of Constantinople from whom he was descended.

The feudal system in Russia
During the second half of the sixteenth century, the feudal system, which was breaking up in Western Europe, started to spread through Russia. The Tsars issued *ukases*, or laws, ordering the peasants not to leave the lands where they lived and making them the property of the landowners. While the Russian peasants were being turned into serfs, west Europeans were experiencing the Renaissance—the so-called 'rebirth of learning', the Reformation—the quarrel between the Protestants and Roman Catholics—and the Reception, the revival in the use of Roman law. Once again, the Russians were excluded from experiences which did much to shape modern European culture.

The Romanovs
When Ivan the Terrible's family died out, Michael Romanov was elected Tsar. Under the Romanovs, westernization was encouraged. In an effort to include Russia in the mainstream of European life, the Romanovs persuaded large numbers of Western craftsmen, artists and scholars to settle in Russia and teach their skills to the local people. For example, Alexis I, father of Peter the Great, was fascinated by all things Western and used to visit the home of one of his counsellors frequently so he could see 'all the wondrous, half-forbidden novelties of the West: painted ceilings, rich pile carpets, ingenious clocks, and pictures by French and German artists'. Peter the Great (1689–1725) started a series of State industries in the hope that his people would follow suit, but with little success. Most of these industries declined and had to be revived by his successors.

Peter the Great also built a new capital which was named St Petersburg, on the shores of the Baltic. This 'northern Venice' was a mixture of luxury and poverty: 'The numerous churches, the monasteries, and noblemen's and gentlemen's houses, the spires, cupolas and crosses

Peter the Great supervising the building of the new capital of St Petersburg, which became a city containing extremes of luxury and poverty.

Feudal life in the country remained largely unchanged for centuries.

at the top of the churches, which are gilded and painted over, makes the city look to be one of the most beautiful and rich in the world ... but upon a nearer view, you will find yourself deceived and disappointed.'

Russian peasants
While the life of the Russian aristocracy and townspeople gradually changed, that of the country people remained largely unaltered. The peasants worked with sickle and scythe to harvest the crops. Their low-lying thatched huts were made of wattle and daub. Inside, a large stove took up 'a third of the room. You bake bread in it. You sleep on top of it. You get inside and take a steam bath in it.' Manners

Peasants complained that the priests took money from the living and from the dead, in funeral expenses.

were simple: 'The women brought in a big bowl of cabbage soup, and for each person a wooden spoon. Everyone was supposed to dip his soup from the common bowl ... When the first bowl was empty, they brought a second full of porridge. It was followed by a bowl of baked raisins.' This was a feast. Normally, the peasants lived in the depth of poverty, close to starvation.

This agricultural world was dominated by all-powerful landlords and priests. Many landlords treated their peasants with complete contempt. Here is a short extract from a typical conversation. Some peasants ask a favour of their landlord: 'Ivan Ivanovich, be gracious, you are our father, and we are your children.' The landlord replied, 'Now enough, enough. You are blockheads—blockheads all round.'

Gradually, the peasants came to resent this kind of treatment. Angrily, they complained that the priests were no better: 'The priest takes from the living [the tithe] and from the dead [funeral expenses].'

This was Mother Russia, a land where little ever happened to disrupt the unchanging life of rich and poor alike.

2 WHAT IS TO BE DONE?

Any country with a small aristocracy and a vast population of landless labourers can expect disorder sooner or later. Russia was no exception. As early as 1606–07, Ivan Bolotnikov, a former serf, led the first peasants' uprising in Russian history. It began in the northern Ukraine and spread rapidly to other parts of Russia before the Boyars, the landlords, put it down in a sea of blood. Stenka Razin led a similar revolt in 1670–71 but with no more success. The third and most serious of the risings was headed by Emilian Pugachev in 1773–75. This time the peasants came close to overthrowing the feudal aristocracy. Eventually, however, Pugachev was captured and executed.

In 1773 Pugachev proclaimed himself to be the husband of Catherine the Great, although the Tsar had been assassinated.

Revolutionary ideas

No sooner had the peasant movement been defeated than the Russian aristocracy started to be affected by the teachings of the European philosophers, who believed in improving the lot of the common people. In 1790, a Russian called Alexander Radishchev, published an important book called *A Journey from St Petersburg to Moscow*, in which he called for the abolition of the aristocracy and serfdom. As a result he was sentenced to be quartered, but was pardoned by Catherine the Great (1762–96) and sent into exile. By the end of the eighteenth century, criticism of serfdom was a frequent theme in Russian literature.

The destruction of Moscow. Napoleon Bonaparte thought that if he could conquer Russia he would be master of the world. Instead, the harsh Russian winter destroyed the French Armies.

Napoleon invades Russia

The French Emperor Napoleon Bonaparte's expansionist ideas brought him into conflict with Russia. In 1811, he boasted: 'In five years I shall be master of the world; only Russia is left and I shall crush her.' However, his invasion of Russia was a gigantic mistake as 'General Frost'—the appallingly cold Russian winter—destroyed the flower of the French armies. But Russia's involvement in the Napoleonic wars had some unexpected results. 'With the return of the Russian armies to their country,' wrote Turgenev, the famous novelist, 'liberal ideas began to spread in Russia.'

The Decembrists

It has been argued that the Russian Revolution has its origin in the Decembrist revolt. This uprising broke out when Tsar Alexander I died in 1825. A group of Guards Officers attempted to seize control of St Petersburg, but, lacking a clear plan, they were eventually surrounded and forced to surrender. Nicholas I, the new Tsar, had their leaders imprisoned, exiled, or executed.

In December 1825, a group of army officers attempted to seize control of St Petersburg. They were surrounded and forced to surrender.

Alexander II implemented many much-needed reforms, such as abolishing serfdom.

Alexander II, the 'Tsar Liberator'
Even though the new Tsar put down any signs of disagreement with ruthless severity, opposition to the régime continued to grow. His successor, Alexander II, decided to satisfy his discontented people by passing much-needed reforms. In 1861, for instance, he gave the serfs their freedom. 'Better,' he said, 'to abolish serfdom from above than wait for it to abolish itself from below.' Later, he established a system of law courts and popularly-elected councils in towns and villages. At first, some reformers led by Alexander Herzen supported the 'Tsar Liberator'. Soon, however, they became dissatisfied with the narrowness of his reforms and turned to creating a revolutionary peasant movement.

Bakunin

Mikhail Bakunin (1814–76), an anarchist, wanted to destroy the State and divide society up into natural units. He believed the peasants should own the land they tilled, as the industrial workers should own the factories and workshops they laboured in. His friend Nicholas Tchemishevsky (1828–89) painted an unforgettable picture of this ideal life

Mikhail Bakunin believed that the State should be destroyed and the land divided up and among the peasants.

in his novel, *What is to be Done?*. In 1861–62, a secret society called *Zemya i Volya* (Land and Freedom) tried to overthrow the Tsarist régime without success. Undaunted, Bakunin and Tchemishevsky founded the *Narodnichestvo*, (The Cult of the People). Their goal was revolution, not reform. They demanded that a national assembly be set up and freedom of speech granted to all.

Such propaganda brought with it a violent official reaction. Alexander II employed police spies and informers to identify the ringleaders whom he imprisoned or sent into exile. In 1866, a young student called Karakozov tried to shoot the Tsar. This outrage led to an even more repressive régime.

The revolution approaches
The seventies witnessed a wave of idealism when thousands of students, teachers and even repentent nobles went out to the peasants preaching revolution. Although this had little effect, it led to the foundation of two groups in 1879: *Cherny Peredel* (The Black Partition), and the *Narodnaya Volya* (The People's Will). The gradual increase in violence made Alexander II rethink his policy and in 1881 he was considering a project for associating elected representatives with legislation, i.e. law making. But on 1 March, the very day he signed the project, the carriage in which he was travelling was blown up by members of 'The People's Will' and he died without being able to establish the new constitution.

Marxism in Russia
Alexander III, the new Tsar, cancelled the project and set about stamping out all opposition to the autocracy. In despair the disappointed revolutionaries turned to Marxism. Karl Marx (1818–83) was a German political philosopher who founded modern communism. He believed the urban working classes all over the world would rise up and overthrow capitalism and replace it with socialism. In a socialist state all citizens would be equal and would own the land, the factories, the means of transport and everything else. His ideas were introduced into Russia by G. V. Plekhanov (1857–1918) who startled his friends in 1889 by predicting: 'The Russian revolution will triumph as a proletarian revolution, or it will not triumph at all.' As Russia was still basically an agricultural country, there seemed little chance of his prediction coming true.

At first most Marxists were students or members of the middle classes. Many of them, like Vladimir Ilyich Lenin, were forced to live in exile out of reach of the Tsarist secret police. Among themselves these exiles debated fiercely on points of principle. In fact, at a meeting in London in 1903, the Russian Marxists quarrelled so badly they

Karl Marx was the German political philosopher who founded the theory which is the basis of modern communism.

Vladimar Lenin was forced for many years to live in exile, away from the Tsarist secret police.

divided into two groups: the Bolsheviks or 'Majorityites' and the Mensheviks or 'Minorityites'. They quarrelled over what kind of party they should create. The Mensheviks believed that they could achieve a socialist state through normal political means, but the Bolsheviks (led by Lenin) thought that the party should be a small revolutionary élite owing absolute obedience to its leadership.

Lenin claimed: 'That no movement can be durable without a stable organization of leaders to maintain continuity; That the more widely the masses are drawn into the struggle and form the basis of the movement, the more it is necessary to have such an organization and the more stable it must be; That the organization must consist chiefly of persons engaged in revolution as a profession; That in a country with despotic government, the more we restrict the membership of this organization to those who are engaged in revolution as a profession ... the more difficult it will be to catch the organization; and the wider will be the circle of men and women of the working class or of other classes of society able to join the movement.'

These revolutionaries awaited the opportunity to transform theory into practice.

3 GROWING PAINS

The Romanov Tsars tried to change Russia from an agricultural into an industrial country. For centuries Russia trailed in the economic wake of other European countries, but during the nineteenth century a belated industrial revolution took place. Between 1861 and

Foundry workers in an iron and steel works in the late nineteenth century Russia.

The rapid development of rail transport greatly increased trade links both internally and to foreign countries.

Low pay meant inadequate housing. In some cases people who could not afford to rent a bed in a hostel slept underneath, on the floor.

1891, the production of cotton goods in the Moscow area alone rose fourfold; coal production in the Donetz Basin increased by 800 per cent; a new oil industry grew up at Baku which was producing 10 million tonnes of oil a year by 1900; the iron industry developed just outside St Petersburg.

This industrial boom was due at least in part to a transport revolution. By 1861 there were only 1,500 kilometres of railway in Russia, but by 1881 there were 23,000 kilometres of track. During the 1890s the Trans-Siberian Railway was laid down, linking European Russia to the Pacific Ocean seaboard. Between 1871 and 1891, internal trade tripled and foreign trade increased two and a half times. As a rapidly developing country Russia attracted investments from the British, French and Germans.

The rise of the proletariat
The industrial revolution led to the growth of the Russian towns and the rise of a proletariat of industrial workers. Most Russian artisans worked in very large factories where they were approached by trade unionists and revolutionaries. According to a British visitor to Russia

Conditions of labour were often grim. The working day often lasted up to twelve hours.

in 1906: 'There is growing up in Russia a new factory race ... it already numbers two million ... the food supply is often bad, and the pay very low even if one allows for the lower standard of living in Russia ... The factory system means under the charge of the directors [of a large cotton mill] live 10,000 persons, that is 5,000 workers and their families. For so great a number there must be strict discipline. The workers feel that they are "under the stick". If they shout they are told to stop. This goes on day by day. They get to hate it.'

Working conditions in the foundries, mines, mills and factories were usually appalling. Wages were low and the working day lasted for twelve to fifteen hours. Women and children were still extensively employed. Since there were no safety regulations, accidents often occurred. Employers reduced wages and increased working hours whenever trade was bad. Workers who became involved in trade union or political activities were sacked and blacklisted. A contemporary complained: 'Wages are being reduced by direct acts or by withdrawal of rent allowances, bonuses, etc. The working day is being lengthened ... and overtime and gangwork are becoming practically obligatory ... Workers, particularly class-conscious [politically active] workers, are discharged on trifling pretexts and often without pretext at all. "Blacklisting" is being applied in the most ruthless manner ... The "system" of fines and beating up is in full swing.'

In the circumstances it is hardly surprising that many of the workers joined revolutionary groups.

Russia expands into Asia
Meanwhile, another kind of revolution was taking place in the Russian countryside. Between 1864 and 1887, Russia annexed Central Asia. Russian farmers advanced across the Steppes, the great plains of Asia, as the European settlers did in the North American prairies. The Russian colonists dispossessed the local people, who were nomadic herdsmen, just as the American settlers drove out the Plains Indians. However, there was a sinister objective behind the Russian advance. As a critic described it at the time: 'The imperial advance of Russia was definitely adopted as a substitute for reform at home.'

The plight of the peasants
The emancipation (freeing) of the serfs did not lead to the agricultural revolution the reformers had hoped for. Many landlords continued to run their estates under the 'labour service system', that is, they let the peasants have land in return for labour services on their own estates and rent. Where more modern farming methods were employed, many peasants lost their land and became poor labourers. However, a small but important group of peasants, called *kulaks*,

Women hauling timber rafts on a river. Many peasants lost their land and became poor labourers when modern farming methods were used.

became more prosperous. Nicholas II's advisers were quick to realize that a large group of successful peasants was the best guarantee the régime had against revolution. Well-to-do farmers did not want to lose their land to anyone, be it Emperor or revolutionary. Peter Stolypin, the Emperor's first minister, set up special banks to lend the more successful peasants money with which to buy more land.

Political unrest

In spite of Nicholas II's savage repression of all opposition, the number of strikes rapidly increased. In 1885, for instance, 8,000 textile workers went on strike in Moscow. As a result, hundreds of workers were exiled to Siberia. The Tsar employed spies and informers to mingle with the workers and peasants and report their doings to the police. All kinds of suggestions were put forward for solving the unrest. Vyacheslav Plehve, the hated Minister of the Interior, put forward perhaps the most dangerous: 'a little victorious war will stop the revolutionary tide.'

Two years later, in 1904, Japan attacked Russia and Plehve's theory was put to the test. Unfortunately, the Russian armies were defeated and the Imperial Grand Fleet was sunk at the Battle of Tsushima. Plehve was assassinated and the workers, led by a certain Father Gapon, marched to the Winter Palace in St Petersburg on Sunday 9 January 1905 to ask for reforms. As the workers filed into the square before the palace, troops opened fire, killing and wounding 1,000 people. 'Little boys who had climbed the trees to watch what was going on were shot down like birds.' Next day, the horrified Gapon wrote, 'We no longer have a Tsar. Today, a river of blood divides him from the Russian people.'

Many lives were lost during the Russo-Japanese war. Although the Russians fought hard they were eventually defeated.

In 1905 troops opened fire on a group of demonstrators led by Father Gapon outside the Winter Palace. Over 1,000 people were killed or badly injured.

Rioters trapped in a courtyard were ruthlessly shot down by the soldiers, despite their pleas for mercy.

The 1905 revolution

'Bloody Sunday', as it became known, led to a full-scale revolution. Hundreds of thousands of workers went on strike. Even the armed forces showed signs of serious discontent. For example, the crew of the battleship *Potemkin* mutinied and sought asylum in Roumania. Soviets—that is, assemblies of freely-elected representatives of workers, peasants and soldiers—were set up in St Petersburg and Moscow, led by Leon Trotsky and Lenin respectively.

In the face of these disorders, the Tsar made peace with Japan and reluctantly issued the October Manifesto promising the Russians a *Duma*, or Parliament. Although the Tsar honoured his promise, he had no intention of giving up his power, as he showed by issuing the Fundamental Laws. One of these declared: 'The All-Russian Emperor possesses the supreme autocratic power. Not only fear and conscience, but God himself, commands obedience to his authority.'

'1905,' asserted Lenin, 'ploughed the soil deeply and uprooted the prejudices of centuries; it awakened millions of workers and tens of millions of peasants to political life and political struggle.'

4 END OF AN ERA

In 1912 the Romanovs celebrated three hundred years of rule. Festivities took place all over Russia. The Tsar's Imperial train was welcomed enthusiastically wherever it appeared. Plays, ballets, and operas were performed to mark the event. Fabergé, the Imperial jewellers, produced all kinds of beautiful and vastly expensive knick-nacks for the rich and famous to give each other. The glorious streets of St Petersburg were lined with cheering crowds.

As the Romanovs celebrated 300 years of rule, poverty dominated most of Russia.

Nevertheless all was not well. The slums of St Petersburg and the other Russian towns were larger than ever. Disease and poverty still dominated countryside and town. The new constitution had made little difference. As soon as the *Duma* showed any independence of thought, it was dissolved. The Emperor's ministers were more famous for their manners than for their intelligence.

Tsar Nicholas II, his wife Alexandra and their haemophiliac son Alexis, (held by a Cossack) see the crowds at the Romanov celebrations.

Rasputin (seated), with some of his admirers. The Tsarina Alexandra relied heavily on his powers to help her son.

The Empress and Rasputin

The Empress Alexandra was the subject of gossip. At last, in 1904, she had borne the Emperor Nicholas a long-awaited son and heir, Alexis. But joy soon turned to anxiety when it was discovered that the Tsarovich suffered from haemophilia, which meant that his blood did not clot properly after injury. The slightest knock caused internal bleeding and the most terrible agony.

The only person who seemed able to help the little boy was Gregory Rasputin, a rascally preacher with hypnotic powers. He was able to calm the child so that his body's ordinary defences could cope with the bleeding. The Tsarina, a powerful personality, was sure that

Russian peasants dig trenches to the rear of the front line during the First World War.

Rasputin has been sent by God to help her stricken son. She would not hear a word against the charlatan, who was notorious for his evil living. As early as 1912, the Dowager Empress Marie Fedorovna prophesied: 'My poor daughter-in-law does not perceive that she is ruining both the dynasty [the royal family] and herself.'

The First World War
While the Romanovs worried about their son, the First World War broke out. At first the war seemed to be the saving of the régime. Just before hostilities began, a member of the *Duma* suggested that the Government and the *Duma* were 'two hostile camps' and that many

Women soldiers were used to boost the war effort. Here the women are blessed by the head of the Church before their departure for the front. They were called the shock battalion.

deputies wanted 'a federal democratic republic on the basis of radical reform'. At that time there had been serious street fighting in St Petersburg, when the workers demanded an eight-hour day and other reforms. The outbreak of war changed all this, uniting the nation against a common enemy.

Defeat

At first all went well. 'The Russian steamroller', as the Allies called the Imperial army, smashed its way into eastern Germany. The Germans, however, rallied and defeated the Russians at the terrible battles of Tannenburg and the Masurian Lakes. Russian casualties were enormous. Soon, the Imperial armies were in full retreat. The war cruelly exposed the Government's weaknesses. Money for essentials such as hospitals, munitions and uniforms had to be raised by public

Russians surrender at the terrible battle of Tannenberg.

By the summer of 1915, the Russian army had suffered one set-back after another. The demoralised soldiers questioned the point of a war that resulted in millions of deaths.

A mutilated Russian soldier returns from the Front to find his family fled and his home destroyed.

subscription. The Tsar spent his entire fortune in this way. The communication system collapsed under the strain. Lack of rolling stock prevented the movement of much-needed food and fuel to the starving, frozen towns.

Defeat followed defeat in spite of the courage of the Russian soldiers; many of whom had no weapons until an armed comrade was killed or wounded. As the Russians retreated they destroyed all the buildings and crops to prevent them falling into enemy hands. As a result the local people had to flee before their own army. The Government had neither the means nor the will to do anything for these refugees. The morale of the Russian nation fell lower and lower.

The death of Rasputin
In these circumstances, Nicholas II made himself Commander-in-Chief of the Imperial Armed Forces and moved to army headquarters at the Front, leaving his wife, the Tsarina Alexandra, in charge of the civil government. This was a great mistake. Nicholas had no military talent, and Alexandra was hated as a German by birth and was blamed for all Nicholas's mistakes. Although Alexandra worked loyally for a Russian victory, she was still dominated by Rasputin.

At last a group of the nobility decided to poison 'the mad monk'. Prince Youssoupoff invited him to his palace at Petrograd (as St Petersburg was now known) to meet his wife. On arrival, Rasputin was given cakes and wine laced with cyanide. When the poison had no effect, Youssoupoff shot him from point-blank range. 'With a violent movement Rasputin jumped to his feet,' Youssoupoff later wrote, 'I was horror-stricken. The room resounded with a wild roar. His fingers ... tried to grip me by the throat.' At that moment, the Prince's friends dashed into the room and shot Rasputin again and again. His body was thrown into the frozen River Neva. Unfortunately, Rasputin's death came too late to save the Tsarina's reputation.

Revolution breaks out
In March 1917, prices were rocketing, wages were low. Both food and fuel were in short supply. All the Tsar's friends warned him that revolution was likely. Grand Duke Alexander Michaelovich wrote, 'It is impossible to rule the country without paying attention to the voice of the people.' The Tsar was unmoved and set out for the Front as usual. Before he reached Pskov, the workers of Petrograd rose. The Tsar ordered the Garrison Commander to disperse the demonstrators. In despair, he replied, 'I cannot restore order in the capital.' The soldiers joined the workers in calling for an end to the régime. 'There is no government any more,' lamented the *Duma's* president.

On 15 March, the Tsar abdicated, in favour of his brother Archduke Michael. The Archduke, however, refused the throne, so the leaders of the *Duma* set up a provisional government with Prince Lvov as Premier. The three-hundred-year reign of the Romanovs was over. Once again the people celebrated in the streets, believing that the war would be soon over, prices reduced, wages increased, the land given to the peasants and a democratic republic set up.

In exile in Switzerland, Lenin was surprised by the news of the 'Bourgeois Revolution'. The Bolshevik leaders, most of whom were in exile in Siberia, had had nothing to do with it. However, when the provisional government granted an amnesty to all the political opponents of the previous régime, a stream of leading Bolsheviks including Kamenev, Zinoviev and Stalin returned to Petrograd.

The Tsar paid little attention to the representatives of the Russian people, including priests.

The Revolution occurred at a crucial moment during the First World War. The Germans were nearing exhaustion and needed to eliminate at least one of their enemies. As a result they transported Lenin and other revolutionaries across Germany in a sealed train. When Lenin reached the Finland Station in Petrograd, instead of congratulating the Bolsheviks, he called on them to stop co-operating with the provisional government and work for a socialist revolution: 'We don't need any bourgeois democracy. We don't need any government except the Soviet of Workers', Soldiers' and Peasants' Deputies.'

5 THE NOVEMBER REVOLUTION

Power in Petrograd was divided between the provisional government, in the Winter Palace, and the Soviet, which sat in the Smolny Institute. Membership of the Petrograd Soviet, and thousands of others like it all over Russia, consisted of freely-elected representatives of the workers, peasants and armed forces. Prince Lvov, the Premier, commented ruefully, 'the Government had authority without power, while the Soviet enjoyed power without authority'.

At this time the Soviets were dominated by Mensheviks and Socialist Revolutionaries. The Socialist Revolutionaries were the descendants of the revolutionary peasants' parties of the '70s and '80s. The Bolsheviks were of little importance. All this was soon to change.

Women demanding change meet in the people's Duma *at Petrograd. The banners read 'Rights for Women' and 'Women Unite'.*

Workers held many protest demonstrations against the provisional government. These demonstrators are carrying a banner demanding a democratic republic.

Failures of the provisional government
From the start the provisional government failed to appreciate the need for immediate reform. Although the cabinet was reorganized to include Mensheviks and Socialist Revolutionaries, little was done to satisfy the people's needs. No move was made to grant the peasants land. The industrial workers' wages still lagged far behind prices. When Alexander Kerensky became Premier in July, Lenin sneered, 'The Kerensky Government is revolutionary in name only. They promise bread, but the speculators still hold it.'

During a demonstration, in July 1917 troops loyal to the provisional government opened fire and killed and wounded hundreds of civilians.

The provisional government's next mistake was to continue the war. Under pressure from Britain and France, the government agreed to make yet another massive military effort. The July offensive, however, was a complete disaster. Eyewitnesses reported, 'In thousands the soldiers were throwing down their guns and streaming from the Front. Like plagues of locusts they came, clogging railways, highways and waterways.' No officer was safe from the furious soldiers: 'At the Front, General Dukhonin was dragged from his carriage and torn to pieces.'

When the news of the military disaster reached the civilian population, there were huge demonstrations, often led by Bolsheviks. Troops loyal to the provisional government opened fire and killed or wounded hundreds. Lenin had to flee to Finland and the Bolshevik newspaper *Pravda* was closed down. The provisional government claimed that this 'July Revolution' was a Bolshevik plot to seize power and that the Bolsheviks were paid by the Germans. Kerensky, the new Premier, seemed to have triumphed. However, danger immediately threatened from a new direction.

The Kornilov affair

General Vladimir Kornilov, the Commander-in-Chief of the Russian armies, believed further revolution could only be avoided by strong leadership from himself. He intended to seize control of Petrograd with the aid of the army. 'It's time,' the General said, 'to hang the German supporters and spies, with Lenin at their head, and to disperse the Soviet of Workers and Soldiers' Deputies so that it will never re-assemble.' Kerensky ordered Kornilov to surrender his command. He refused and advanced on Petrograd at the head of his troops. In this emergency, Kerensky opened the arsenals and armed every able-bodied man who was prepared to fight the General. As a result the Bolsheviks, led by Leon Trotsky, emerged from hiding and set to work fortifying not only Petrograd but their own position.

Kerensky, who became the Premier of the provisional government in July 1917.

This still from a Russian film shows the shots being fired from the Aurora *towards the Winter Palace in Petrograd, signalling the start of the Uprising*

A special 'Committee for Struggle with Counter-Revolution' was formed containing Bolsheviks, Mensheviks and Socialist Revolutionaries. Representatives were sent to Kornilov's army. The troops deserted their commander, who was captured and disgraced. Once again, Kerensky had triumphed but only by placing arms in the hands of the Bolshevik Red Guards.

The Bolshevik Revolution
All these disasters—the military defeats, the food and fuel shortages, the lack of reform and the civil disorders—lowered the reputation of the provisional government. Everyone warned: 'The influence of Bolshevik ideas is spreading very rapidly. There is general weariness, an irritability and a desire for peace at any price.' To have any chance of staying in power, Kerensky had to attack and destroy the Bolsheviks. This he feared to do.

While he wavered, the Bolsheviks, particularly the golden-tongued Trotsky, were working hard on the Petrograd garrison. Trotsky won the support of the sailors at the Kronstadt naval station just outside the city, and that of the troops holding the great fortress of St Peter

Leon Trotsky was a persuasive speaker and military leader, who persuaded many workers to fight for the Bolsheviks.

and St Paul within Petrograd itself. Lenin, who had now returned from exile, decided the time was ripe for the Bolsheviks to seize power. 'Having obtained a majority of the Soviet of Workers' and Soldiers' Deputies,' he argued, 'the Bolsheviks can and must take power into their own hands.' A Military Revolutionary Committee was set up with Trotsky at its head. On the night of 6 November 1917, the Bolshevik crew of the cruiser *Aurora*, and the soldiers in the fortress of St Peter and St Paul, fired the shots which were the signal for the rising.

A street scene in Petrograd during 1917. Bolsheviks block the end of a street with an armoured car.

Companies of Red Guards occupied the main post office, the telephone exchange, the banks and the railway and power stations. At the same time other detachments surrounded the Winter Palace, the headquarters of the provisional government. In fact this imposing institution fell with little opposition. The soldiers started to loot the Palace until a Red Guard bellowed: 'Come, Comrades, let's show that we're not thieves and bandits. Everybody out of the Palace except the Commissars [the political officers] until we get sentries posted.'

The Bolsheviks triumphant
Kerensky escaped and led an army against Petrograd, but when the troops came face to face with the revolutionaries, they deserted to their side so that Kerensky had to flee the country. Many Bolsheviks hoped Lenin would create a coalition government of all the socialist parties at this time, but he and Trotsky insisted that a purely Bolshevik cabinet should be formed: 'We won't give an inch. If there are Comrades here who haven't the courage ... let them leave with the rest of the cowards and conciliators. Backed by the workers and the soldiers we shall go on.' A Council of People's Commissars was set up with Lenin as President.

As yet, the Bolsheviks represented only a small minority of the revolutionaries, let alone the people of Russia. Could they retain power? Lenin had no doubts. 'We shall now proceed to construct the Socialist order,' he promised.

6 ALL POWER TO THE SOVIETS

During their first few months in power, the Bolshevik Council of People's Commissars issued a steady stream of decrees. They abolished class, titles of nobility, and ranks in the armed forces. All people were declared equal no matter what their race, sex or religion. The land, industry, commerce and the banks were nationalized. The peasants took over the land and workers' committees organized the factories. The Bolsheviks regarded religion with contempt and thought marriage outmoded, but placed a high value on education.

Chaos and civil war
However, conditions were appalling. Russia starved and military expeditions had to be sent to the countryside to sieze the peasants' stock. Law and order collapsed. Burglaries, hold-ups and murders increased dramatically. The poor forcibly occupied the homes of the better-off. If the Bolsheviks' paper promises were to be turned into realities, they had to have time and peace. To the open dismay of many of his followers, Lenin insisted that Russia must make peace on any terms.

After the allied occupation, Russians marched through Archangel, raising forces to overthrow the Bolsheviks.

Victims of the Bolsheviks. Both Whites and Reds were responsible for the murder and ill-treatment of thousands of innocent people.

The Allies had been horrified by the news of the November Revolution and feared that if the Bolsheviks were successful, workers everywhere would rise up and seize control of their countries. Consequently, British and French troops were landed at Archangel and Murmansk while the Japanese occupied Eastern Siberia. The Allies actively encouraged White (Royalist) Generals to raise armies to overthrow the Red Bolsheviks. Soon the Bolsheviks found themselves fighting a vicious civil war.

Terror
Disturbances and disagreements spread all over Russia and the survival of Bolshevism was in great doubt. In this emergency, Lenin acted ruthlessly. The All-Russian Extraordinary Commission to Fight Counter-Revolution, Sabotage and Speculation, i.e. the secret police or *Cheka*, was established 'to seek out, arrest and shoot immediately [anybody] connected ... with counter-revolutionary agitators.' In the ensuing 'Red Terror', many thousands of innocent people were murdered. When his friends complained of the excesses, Lenin snarled: 'Do you really think we shall be victorious without using the most cruel terror?' Similar methods were employed by the Whites who became infamous for 'Shooting tens of thousands of workers, flogging peasants of entire districts. Public flogging of women. The absolutely unbridled power of the officers and young squires. Endless looting.' As a result, most Russians came to see the Bolsheviks as the defenders of the mother country against the traitorous Whites who were in league with the foreign invaders.

The closing of the Constituent Assembly

On 18 January 1918, the long-awaited Constituent Assembly met. The elections which had been held in the previous November were a resounding defeat for the Bolsheviks. Of the 710 seats, the Socialist Revolutionaries obtained 410, the Bolsheviks 175, the Kadets (Liberals) 17 and the Mensheviks 16. At 4 pm on the first day, Red Guards told the Chairman of the Assembly: 'It's time to quit. The guards are tired.' When the members returned the following day, they found the Assembly hall locked. The Constituent Assembly never met again. Lenin had no intention of yielding power even to democratically-elected representatives.

Treaty of Brest Litovsk

In the same month, Trotsky set off for Brest Litovsk to negotiate peace terms with the Germans. Their demands were so high that even Trotsky believed Russia had no option but to fight on. Lenin, however, was adamant. Peace must be made at any cost. 'The Russian Revolution must sign the peace,' he explained, 'to obtain a breathing space to recuperate for the struggle to come.' By the treaty signed in March, Russia lost a quarter of its population, two-thirds of its best agricultural land and three-quarters of its coal and iron resources.

Russian leaders at the time the peace treaty was signed at Brest Litovsk. Russia bought peace by losing two-thirds of her best land and three quarters of her coal and iron resources.

The death of the Tsar

In the meantime, the civil war favoured first one side and then the other. In July 1918, White forces approached Ekaterinburg in Siberia, where the Tsar Nicholas II and his family were imprisoned. The local Bolsheviks panicked. According to the official account on 16 July, the garrison commander told the Tsar: 'Your men have tried to save you, but haven't succeeded, and we are forced to put you to death.' He immediately raised his revolver and fired point-blank at the Tsar, killing him instantly. His wife, his four daughters and the Tsarovich were also shot. Their bodies were cut up, burned, drenched with acid and the remains dropped down an abandoned mine shaft.

The Tsar Nicholas II in captivity. He and his family were later moved to Ekaterinburg, where they were executed.

White Guards during the bitter Civil War which followed the Revolution.

The fighting continues
Shortly afterwards, the tension between the socialist parties reached breaking point. A Socialist Revolutionary called Fanya Kaplan shot and seriously wounded Lenin. The Bolshevik Government ordered an end to 'this clemency and slackness. All Right Socialist Revolutionaries known to local Soviets are to be arrested immediately. From among the bourgeoisie and the officers, large numbers of hostages are to be seized.' The 'Red Terror' deepened.

Trotsky, the Commissar for War, strengthened the Red Army and beat back the Whites in all directions. General Yudenich was smashed before Petrograd, General Deniken's army collapsed, forces led by Admiral Kolchak were driven back to the Pacific coastline and Baron Wrangel fled to the Crimea. When the Poles invaded the Ukraine, they were routed by the Bolsheviks, led by Tukhachevsky. The Reds advanced on Warsaw and a thrill of terror went through the West. The Europeans feared that the Bolshevik success would lead to a mass uprising of the workers. However, to their relief, the Bolsheviks were defeated at the Battle of the Vistula and made peace with the Poles.

At the beginning of Bolshevik rule, poverty and starvation haunted the Russians.

Discontent continues

Although Russia was purged of counter-revolutionaries, the life of the ordinary Russian was still grindingly hard. The towns were short of food and fuel. Housing was a greater problem than ever. Many drainage and communication systems had broken down. Cholera and typhus swept through the population. Most of the workers' committees had failed. Wages were lower than ever. Petrograd's population had fallen from 2,500,000 to 500,000. The workers, peasants and armed forces were angry and disillusioned. Was this the socialist state they had fought for? The remaining Socialist Revolutionaries and Mensheviks appeared in the streets and demanded change.

The Kronstadt Rising

The sailors at Kronstadt shared these feelings and rose in revolt in 1921, declaring: 'In view of the fact that the present Soviets do not express the will of the workers and peasants,' the Government should, 'immediately hold new elections by secret ballot.' The Bolshevik leaders ordered an immediate attack on Kronstadt. The sailors, who had played such an important part in the Bolshevik Revolution, were slaughtered. A contemporary wrote: 'Distant rumbling reaches my ears as I cross the Nevsky [the main street in Petrograd]. It sounds again, stronger and nearer, as if rolling towards me. All at once I realize that artillery is being fired ... Kronstadt has been attacked. My heart is numb with despair. Something has died within me.'

7 AN ERA OF TRANSITION

By 1921, the Russian people were at the end of their tether. Lenin showed his genius and adaptability by ending his policy of War Communism and replacing it with the New Economic Policy (NEP). He admitted: 'Our poverty and ruin are so great we cannot hope to restore large-scale factory state socialist production at a stroke ... Hence, it is necessary to a certain extent, to help to restore small industry ... the effect will be the revival of the petty bourgeoisie and of capitalism on the basis of a certain amount of free trade.'

Women bartering the necessities of life in Petrograd, 1922.

As this statement suggests, Lenin allowed small businessmen, called *'nepmen'*, to start up factories and shops while insisting that all large-scale manufacture be run by the State. The farmers were also allowed to sell their goods on the open market if they wanted to. Lenin hoped to convince his people of the superiority of the socialist system by the success of the State factories and farms.

Problems of the NEP period
Lenin found it very difficult to change problems in the workplace: apathy and absenteeism were frequent, as they had been in pre-revolutionary days. On the other hand, the schools and universities were crammed to overflowing. No entrance qualifications were required; everybody had the right to attend. After the gloomy days of the Revolution and Civil War, the arts flourished once more. 'The comparative

People who had never been to a school filled classes to overflowing.

Homeless children register at a school set up for orphans. Russia's struggles left many children without parents.

tolerance of the NEP period had invigorated the Soviet theatre,' wrote a visitor. 'With few exceptions the finest things in post-revolutionary Russian drama, cinema and dance belonged to that time.' Equality was the order of the day. Wages and salaries were the same for all workers no matter what kind of post they held. There was little variety. Most homes had the same kind of furniture and equipment. Unless citizens could afford the *nepmen's* high prices, they had to be content with the cheap goods available from the State stores.

An American living in Russia at this time commented: 'The private shops were higher-priced than their government competitors next door—they had to meet the staggering taxes. But they had more and better merchandise, and exerted themselves to please the customers. By contrast the official stores were pitifully poor, crude and unprofitable.'

Visitors to Russia in the 1920s soon discovered that: 'Our chief personal problem, as that of every other permanent resident, was housing ... Flats that formerly housed one family now contained half a dozen,

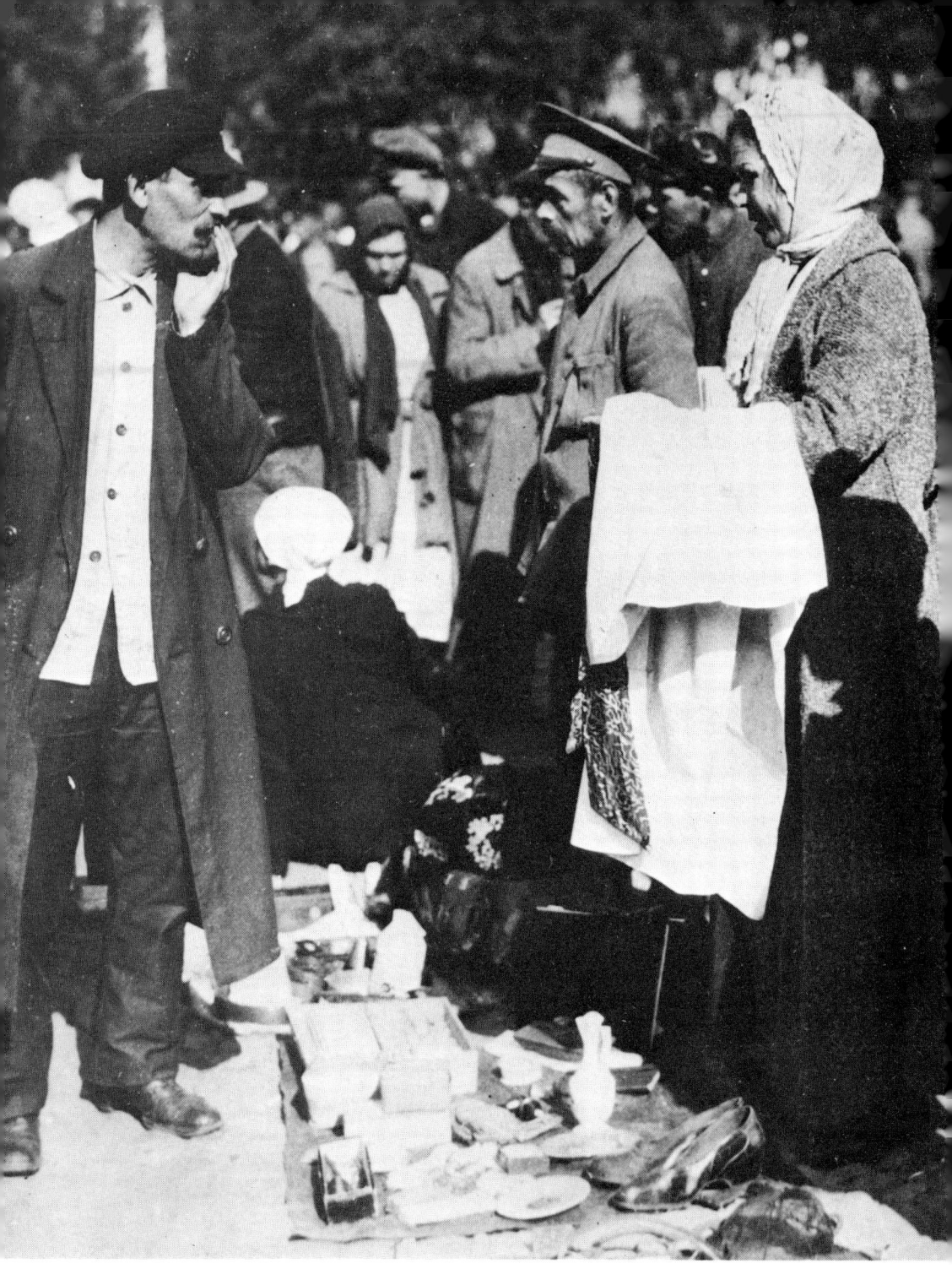

A once-wealthy woman tries to sell some of her possessions in the street.

with an overflow of "house workers" [servants] sleeping on boxes in the corridor, on the kitchen floor, on the common stove ... People married and divorced, lied and denounced their neighbours, for a little space ... In the midst of this hideous overcrowding, however, many privileged officials, police officers, and particularly *nepmen* had managed to acquire the luxury of entire apartments of two or more rooms.'

Capitalism and socialism

The NEP period was at best an armed truce. The compromise with capitalism was loathed by most dedicated Communists. The *nepmen* were despised and insulted by the people and opposed by the government, who taxed them savagely but without destroying them. This large bourgeois class had no political power, no culture of its own and no respect. In Moscow, the situation was clearly seen on the Tverskaya, or main street: 'Along its length were private stores, state shops, private restaurants, gypsy cellars, the government-operated casino, private peddlers, beggars and prostitutes, the offices of State trusts and the headquarters of the leading newspapers.'

This main street was a symbol of Russia's half-socialist, half-capitalist state. People like Trotsky were impatient to attack the *nepmen* and *kulaks*. He called for a speedy, planned industrialization of the country.

Lenin and Stalin

During the NEP period a tremendous struggle for political power was taking place. Lenin's health had collapsed and he experienced a series of strokes. In spite of his illness, however, he continued to take a lively interest in affairs. One of the younger Bolshevik leaders, Joseph Stalin, had gradually worked his way into power. Although Lenin approved his appointment as General Secretary of the Communist Party, he did not fully trust him and tried to counterbalance his influence by offering Trotsky the post of Deputy Chairman of the Council of People's Commissars. Trotsky, however, declined.

As Stalin's power increased, he allowed his arrogance to become visible and he made the mistake of insulting Lenin's wife on a series of occasions when her husband was very ill and expected to die. Lenin recovered and started to dictate a Political Testament in which he recommended that Stalin be removed from his post.

Lenin died on 21 January 1924, before he could launch his attack on Stalin. As Trotsky was also ill and away from the capital, Stalin was able to stage-manage the state funeral and present himself to the Russian nation as Lenin's natural heir. 'Ours is the only country,' he boasted, 'where the crushed and labouring masses have succeeded in throwing off the rule of the landlords and capitalists. You know,

Lenin did not trust Stalin (right), although the two men appear to be friendly here.

Comrades, and the whole world now admits it, that this gigantic struggle was led by Comrade Lenin.' Other foreign commentators, such as Winston Churchill, were less enthusiastic. 'Their worst misfortune was his [Lenin's] birth,' wrote Churchill; 'the next worse, his death.'

The rise of Stalin
At the time of Lenin's death, the Politburo (the ruling committee of the Communist Party) contained Trotsky, Zinoviev, Kamenev, Bukharin and Rykov, all great Bolshevik leaders. By 1938, they were all dead or, in the case of Trotsky, in exile.

With great cunning, Stalin played the members of the 'Old Guard' off against each other. First, he made common cause with Zinoviev and Kamenev to bring down Trotsky, whom they distrusted. Then, he broke Zinoviev and Kamenev with the help of the moderate Bukharin and Rykov. Finally, he turned on Bukharin and Rykov and drove them from power. Supreme at last, Stalin was able to carry out his belief in 'Socialism in One Country', that country being Russia.

Stalin was determined to make Russia not only a model communist state but also the most powerful country in the world. He believed that the capitalist countries of the world were only waiting for a favourable opportunity to attack and destroy Russia. Within Russia itself, he was sure there were thousands of traitors who wanted to bring him down and return to the bad old days. Stalin was determined to crush both the enemy within and the enemy without.

Over 1,000,000 people attended Lenin's funeral. The banner on the right reads; 'Lenin's grave is the cradle of liberty for the people.'

8 STALIN'S REVOLUTION

As undisputed leader of Russia, Stalin introduced the first Five Year Plan (1929–34), arguing: 'We must transform the USSR from a weak, agrarian country ... drive out without mercy the capitalist elements, widen the front of the Socialist form of economy, create the economic basis for the abolition of classes in the USSR, create in our country an industry which would be capable of re-equipping and organizing ... our transport and our agriculture on a socialist basis.'

Agricultural reform

The first thing to be done in Stalin's opinion was 'the liquidation of the *kulaks* as a class' so that their lands could be made into co-operative (*kolhosy*) or state (*sovhosy*) farms. Squads of soldiers and police

Stalin forced many Kulaks *to give up their land, so it could be used for State farms.*

Lunch time on a model collective farm.

enforced this policy. A Communist described such a scene: 'In the background, guarded by soldiers with drawn revolvers, stood about twenty peasants, young and old, with bundles on their backs. A few of them were weeping. The others stood there sullen, resigned, helpless ... As I stood there, distressed, ashamed, helpless, I heard a woman shouting in an unearthly voice ... The woman, her hair streaming, held a flaming sheaf of grain in her hands. Before anyone could reach her, she tossed the burning sheaf onto the thatched roof of the house, which burst into flames instantaneously. "Infidels! Murderers!" the distraught woman was shrieking. "We worked all our lives for our house. You won't have it. The flames shall have it."'

Trainloads of these peasants were deported to the concentration camps in the icy north, the forests, the steppes and the deserts, never to be seen again.

Rather than conform, many peasants slaughtered their animals and burned their stores and crops. As a result, there was a calamitous decline in food production which, coupled with a series of harvest failures, led to famine and epidemic disease. The smallholdings were joined together to form collectives or State farms. A visitor to a state farm saw 'the model stables, the model cattle-sheds, the model pigsties, and especially a gigantic hen-house—the last word in hen houses,' but observed that the workers lived in 'a row of hovels. There, four people share a room measuring eight by six feet ... and have to content themselves with bread supplemented by dried fish.' However, in spite of the killings, deportations and inefficiency, progress was made. Mechanization, for example, was gradually introduced. Motor tractor stations were set up in each area to service the collectives and state farms, for Stalin claimed, 'It was absolutely necessary for Russia, if we were to avoid periodic famines, to plough the land with tractors.'

Industrialization
While the farms were being collectivized, the towns were being industrialized. All industries were set fantastic production targets and no excuses for failure were accepted. As all workers were paid the same wages, a new kind of incentive had to be found to stimulate them to greater efforts. 'Socialist competition between individuals, brigades and whole departments,' it was claimed, 'was unquestionably instrumental in raising production and efficiency.' Gradually, Stalin had to allow bonuses to be paid and special privileges to be granted to outstanding workers. When industries failed to reach the set target, the 'wreckers' responsible were arrested, tried and imprisoned. Stalin was unmoved by the people's suffering. In February 1931 he insisted: 'The pace must not be slackened. On the contrary, we must quicken it as is within our powers.' Progress was made on all fronts.

Despite the model work-places, people still lived in cramped conditions, such as this basement shared by a whole family.

Housing

Housing conditions, for instance, started to improve at last. An American working at the new industrial town of Magnitogorsk wrote of 'the large apartment houses, three, four and five stories high, containing between seventy-five and two hundred rooms each. The houses were brick and stone stuccoed and painted various colours ... They were arranged in long rows, like military barracks ... The metal roofs were painted red and blue. There were balconies in all the houses. Between the houses ran wide streets, with sidewalks, along which many trees had been planted.'

Ten to sixteen year olds were called 'Pioneers' and the pioneer movement still exists today, linking outdoor activities with an academic and political education.

Stalin's dictatorship

Stalin believed in firm social control. In 1935 he reintroduced the death penalty for a variety of offences, for citizens of twelve years of age and above. The discipline in school became much stricter. Examinations were reintroduced and students had to qualify to go to universities or polytechnics. Political training took place alongside academic study. Eight to ten-year-olds became 'Octobrists', ten to sixteen-year-olds 'Pioneers' and nineteen to twenty-three-year-olds became *Komsomolsi*. Divorce and abortion were discouraged, as was attendance at church. All forms of art and literature were carefully censored. A passport system was introduced so that people could be sent wherever their skills were required. A network of spies and informers monitored everybody's actions and statements.

Purges and 'show trials'

When he was ready, Stalin attacked 'his enemies'. Between 1933 and 1934, one million out of a total $2\frac{1}{2}$ million members of the Russian Communist Party were expelled for so-called 'counter-revolutionary and Trotskyite behaviour'. 'Show trials' were stage-managed at which eminent former leaders of the Communist Party—such as Kamenev, Zinoviev, Bukharin and Rykov—stood up in court and confessed to crimes which they quite obviously had not committed, were condemned and executed. Millions of people were sent to concentration camps by the secret police. Even military heroes, such as Marshal Tukhachevsky, were executed as 'German spies'. Finally, the secret police themselves were purged so that they could not tell any of their secrets. When Stalin called a halt to the Terror in 1938, several million people had been 'eliminated' and between 7 and 14 million were left to die in labour camps.

Why did Stalin behave in this way? Many years later, Nikita Khrushchev, who had been one of Stalin's most faithful followers, described his master as 'capricious, irritable and brutal'. 'His persecution mania,' Khrushchev maintained, 'reached unbelievable dimensions.' Stalin trusted no-one and would have continued driving and purging the Russian people without mercy had he not been surprised by the German invasion of Russia in 1941. Stalin then turned his full attention to defeating a real enemy—Hitler and the Nazis.

Stalin's ruthless elimination of several million Russians was only halted by the onset of the Second World War.

9 THE UNFINISHED REVOLUTION

The German invasion of 1941 took Stalin by surprise. The Soviet armies were pushed back until they made a last-ditch stand before Leningrad (as Petrograd is now known), Moscow and Rostov. In spite

The Russians inflicted a severe defeat on the Germans at the Battle of Stalingrad.

Stalingrad in ruins. Over 2 million Russians died in the Second World War.

of appalling suffering and terrible casualties, the Russians held firm and then hit back, defeating the Germans at the Battle of Stalingrad in 1943. Thereafter, triumphant Russian armies liberated Roumania, Bulgaria, Yugoslavia, Czechoslovakia, Hungary and Austria, not to mention Finland, the Baltic States, Poland and East Germany.

When the Second World War came to an end, Stalin held on to these countries and treated them like satellite states. As Winston Churchill described, 'From Stettin on the Baltic to Trieste on the Adriatic, an iron curtain has descended across the continent.' Thereafter, a 'Cold War' was waged between the communist East and the capitalist West.

The death of Stalin

As soon as the Second World War was over, Stalin demanded another industrial and agrarian revolution. 'Our Party,' he insisted, 'intends to organize a new powerful upsurge of the national economy which will enable us to raise the level of our industry threefold compared with the pre-war level.' He also pressed his scientists to produce an atomic bomb so that Russia would be the military equal of the USA. He was as suspicious of his own people as ever and launched a new purge of the Communist Party. When he died, in 1953, most Russians sighed with relief.

Stalin was replaced by the dual leadership of Marshal Bulganin and Nikita Khrushchev. In 1956, Khrushchev denounced Stalin's style of leadership: 'Everything was decided by him alone without any consideration,' he announced.

Khrushchev
Khrushchev himself favoured a more relaxed style. He openly admitted, 'We must help the people eat well, dress well and live well.' 'You cannot put theory in your soup,' he joked, 'or Marxism in your clothes.' Life became less harsh as more attention was paid to ordinary people's needs. An American commented in 1972 that 'roughly 44 million new units of housing have been built since the war ... more than in any other country in the world.' Women have more rights in Russia than elsewhere: 'Abortions are legal. Four-month paid maternity leaves are written into law, and jobs must be kept for new mothers for a year.'

Social problems
Russia suffered from the same kind of social problems as the rest of Europe. 'The *stilyagi* [the Russian version of Teddy boys] are bright young things in revolt against their whole environment and have focused all their inarticulate desires on jive and flashy clothes,' a visitor observed. Hooliganism was also common as a result of 'broken homes, lack of parental discipline and care, orphaning on a very big scale as a result of the war, atrocious housing conditions ... and a sense of frustration and futility.'

Khrushchev made a big effort to solve the agrarian problem that had defeated his predecessors. 'Ostensibly, in the interests of efficiency, he had picked out no fewer than 6,000 Party functionaries from the towns and appointed them as managers of collective farms.' In 1954 he launched 'the Virgin Lands Campaign' to turn vast areas of Kazakhstan and south-west Siberia into rich agricultural land. But, in spite of all his efforts, the farmers still failed to reach their targets and wheat had to be imported from the USA.

Many Communists disapproved of Khrushchev's policies. His 'weakness' led to risings in the satellite states which had to be put down by Russian troops, most notably in Hungary in 1956. His policy of co-existence with the capitalist world led, it was believed, to a decline in respect for the Soviet Union. Then, in 1962, the US President J. F. Kennedy forced Khrushchev to order his men to dismantle rocket installations which they had erected in Cuba. As a result, Khrushchev gradually lost power and was quietly replaced by Leonid Brezhnev and Alexei Kosygin in 1964. These leaders took a harder line towards their own people and the capitalists abroad.

Khrushchev's style of leadership was much more relaxed that Stalin's.

Brezhnev and Kosygin lay a wreath at the monument to Soviet soldiers who died fighting in Hungary in 1956.

Russia under Brezhnev and Kosygin
Under Brezhnev and Kosygin, Russia continued to change. The old Bolshevik belief in equality faded rapidly. 'The privileged class,' remarked an observer, 'is a sizeable chunk of Soviet society—well over a million ... The most conspicuous symbols of rank and privilege are the chauffeur-driven limousines ... Practically every major centre in the Soviet Union ... has special state residences for the élite.' The supply of food and goods changed; self-service stores and pre-packaged foods appeared. 'Their standard of living is improving noticeably,' admitted a foreign visitor in the 1970s, 'but it is still nowhere near the level of the West, especially America, against which Russians are keen to measure themselves.

The satellite countries
In spite of Russia's continuing military might, her satellite countries started to show more independence. President Ceaucescu of Roumania insisted on taking a national rather than a Russian line. In Czechoslovakia, however, attempts to introduce liberal reforms were quashed when Russian troops invaded the country in 1968 and the Czech leaders were expelled from the Communist Party. In Poland, members of the 'illegal' trade union, 'Solidarity', threatened to overthrow the Russian-backed régime. Although they failed, Solidarity has not been completely destroyed and the Polish Government is adopting a softer approach. Relations between

Russia and the USA gradually improved and a number of attempts—the SALT Talks (Strategic Arms Limitation Talks)—were held to reduce the nuclear arms race. For a time, rivalry between the two superpowers seemed to be confined to the exploration of space.

Russia today
After a period of stability, first Kosygin and then Brezhnev died. Westerners feared their deaths would lead to another period of Cold War as their successor, Andrei Andropov, had been the head of the dreaded KGB—the State Political Police. In fact, their fears proved to be groundless as Andropov was a sick man and died in 1983. His replacement, Chernenko, was also old and ill and unable to stamp

Mikhail Gorbachev and President Reagan meeting in 1985 to discuss their economic and military policies.

any pattern on to government policy. On his death in 1985, a much younger man, Mikhail Gorbachev, became First Secretary of the Communist Party of the Soviet Union. People everywhere hoped that his arrival heralded a period of greater harmony between East and West. However, in spite of his charm, Mr Gorbachev made it clear that nothing had changed fundamentally.

Gorbachev's strong objections to the United States 'Star Wars' policy reminded everyone that the Russians believe as deeply as ever in the truth of communism. They may not have achieved all their ideals but they are convinced that theirs is the only path to these goals. On the surface, Russia may look more and more like the rest of Europe, but its culture and beliefs are still very different. As a young Russian told a Western journalist, 'Just because we dig Jimi Hendrix doesn't mean we are less ready to fight for our country.'

The message of these young Russians at an anti-war rally is one that can be understood in every country.

DATE CHART

1825	The Decembrist uprising	1917	The Bourgeois Revolution (March); The July Revolution; The Kornilov Affair; Lenin returns to Russia; The November or Bolshevik Revolution; Council of the People's Commissars
1825–55	Reign of Nicholas I		
1855–81	Reign of Alexander II, the 'Tsar Liberator'		
1861	Emancipation of the serfs		
1866	Assassination attempt on the Tsar		
1877	Rise of the peasant revolutionary groups	1918	Dissolution of the Constituent Assembly; Peace Treaty of Brest-Litovsk (March); Tsar Nicholas II and his family assassinated (July); Formation of Russian Socialist Federative Soviet Republic (July)
1881–94	Reign of Alexander III		
1894–1917	Reign of Nicholas II		
1898	Russian Social Democratic Workers' Party founded in Minsk		
1903	The Social Democrats divide into Bolsheviks and Mensheviks		
1904–05	Russo-Japanese War	1918–20	Russian Civil War
1905	'Bloody Sunday' and the October Manifesto	1921	The Kronstadt Rising; The New Economic Policy (NEP)
1906–11	Peter Stolypin, First Minister; creation of the *kulaks*	1922	Formation of the Union of Soviet Socialist Republics (USSR)
1912–16	'Rule' of Rasputin over Tsarina Alexandra	1924	Death of Lenin Stalin takes power
1914	Outbreak of the First World War	1925	Trotsky driven from power

1927	Kamenev and Zinoviev expelled	1956	Hungarian uprising
1929	Stalin sets up a dictatorship	1962	Cuban Missile Crisis
1929	First Five-Year Plan	1964–82	Leonid Breznev and Kosygin control Russian policy
1936–38	Stalin's Great Purge	1968	Russian invasion of Czechoslovakia
1941	Germany invades Russia	1982	Andropov in power
1943	Russian victory at Stalingrad	1983	Chernenko in power
1945	End of Second World War and start of Cold War	1985	Mikhail Gorbachev becomes First Secretary of Russian Communist Party
1953	Death of Stalin		
1953–64	Nikita Khrushchev dominates the Politburo		Reagan meets Gorbachev

GLOSSARY

Agrarian Relating to the division and cultivation of land.
Amnesty A gneral pardon.
Anarchist A person who believes in abolishing government in favour of voluntary co-operation.
Autocrat A ruler with total, unlimited power.
Ballot A way of voting.
Bourgeoisie The capitalist middle class.
Bolsheviks Of the majority: Lenin's supporters within the Russian Social Democratic Party.
Capitalist A person who has spare money to invest in trade or business and who lives totally or partially upon the profits.
Charlatan Someone who professes to a knowledge he doesn't have.
Cheka The political police set up by Lenin in 1918 to destroy counter-revolutionary forces.
Clemency Showing mercy or leniency.
Cold War Political hostility and military tension between the American and Soviet blocs.

Commissar   A political officer in early Communist Party days, or a member of Lenin's first cabinet, the Council of Commissars.
Communist   The general name for a Marxist-Leninist, adopted by the Bolsheviks in 1918.
Conciliators   People who try to reconcile or make peace.
Decembrists   The liberal revolutionaries who rose against Tsar Nicholas I in December 1825.
Kadets   Constitutional Democrats; they played a prominent part in the *Duma* after 1905 and the provisional government in 1917.
KGB   The present Russian political police organization responsible for espionage and counter-espionage.
Kolhose   A collective farm made up of peasant holdings.
Manifesto   A public declaration of policies.
Marxism   The belief that the urban working classes will rise up and destroy capitalism, replacing it with socialism and a classless society where government will wither away.
Mensheviks   Of the minority; Lenin's critics within the Russian Social Democratic Party.
Narodnik   A believer in the common people; a member of a nineteenth-century revolutionary peasant movement.
NEP   The New Economic Policy adopted by Lenin in 1921 as a half-way house between capitalism and socialism.
Politburo   Policy-making committee of the Russian Communist Party.
Proletariat   The urban working classes whom Marx thought would overthrow capitalism.
Red   A word used to refer to communist or revolutionary groups.
Republic   A constitution without a ruler in the form of a king or emperor, but with some kind of parliamentary system.
Rus   The Viking traders from Scandinavia who gave their name to Russia.
Satellite State   A dependent country.
Socialist Revolutionary Party   The twentieth-century Peasant Revolutionary Socialist Party.
Socialism in One Country   Stalin's belief that the Bolsheviks should give up trying to foment world-wide revolution and concentrate on making Russia a model communist state.
Soviet   A democratically-elected assembly of workers', peasants' and fighting men's representatives.
Sovhose   A Russian State farm.
Subjugate   Bring into submission.
Tsar   The Russian ruler: the word is a form of 'Caesar'.
Ukase   An Imperial decree or law.
USSR   Union of Soviet Socialist Republics.
White   A word used to refer to royalist or anti-revolutionary groups.

FURTHER READING

Histories of the Russian Revolution
Gibson, M. *Russia under Stalin* (Wayland, 1972)
Kochan, L. *The Russian Revolution* (Wayland, 1971)
Halliday, H. E. *Russia in Revolution* (A Cassell Caravel Book, 1967)
Robottom, J. *Modern Russia* (Longmans, 1972)

Biographies
Brown, T. *J. Stalin* (Wayland, 1977)
Kochan, L. *Lenin* (Wayland, 1974)
Smith, W. H. C. *The Last Czar* (Wayland, 1973)
Mack, D. W. *Lenin and the Russian Revolution* (Then and There Books, 1970)

Collections of photographs
Goldston, R. *The Soviets: A Pictorial History of Communist Russia* (Bantam, 1967)
Salisbury, H. E. *Russia in Revolution* 1900–1930 (André Deutsch, 1978)

Contemporary accounts
Almedingen, E. M. *I Remember St Petersburg* (Longmans, 1969)
Krupskaya, N. *Memories of Lenin* (Panther, 1970)
Trotsky, L. *History of the Russian Revolution* (Gollancz, 1970)

Extracts from contemporary documents
Stacey, F. W. *Lenin and the Russian Revolution* (The Archive Series, 1970)
Stacey, F. W. *Stalin and the Making of Modern Russia* (The Archive Series, 1970)

PICTURE ACKNOWLEDGEMENTS

BBC Hulton 5, 6, 8, 10, 12, 15, 20, 27, 29, 30, 33, 37, 45, 47, 48, 49, 51, 54, 57; Imperial War Museum *front cover*; The Mansell Collection 11, 17, 18, 21, 40, 41, 44; Mary Evans Picture Library 4, 43, 46, 56; Novosti Press Agency 14, 19, 20, 22, 24, 28, 31, 32, 34, 35, 38, 39, 42, 50, 52, 53, 58, 62, 64, 65, 67, 68, 69, 70; Wayland Picture Library 9, 14, 25, 59, 61, 63

INDEX

Agriculture 23, 52, 58–9, 60, 66
Alexander I, Tsar 13
Alexander II, Tsar 14, 16
Alexander III, 16
Alexandra, Tsarina 30–31, 36, 48
Alexis, Tsarovich 30–31, 48
Allied occupation 45–6
Andropov, Andrei 69
Army, Russian 27, 32–3, 35–6, 40–44, 50
Asia, expansion into 23
Atomic bomb 69
Aurora 43

Bakunin, Mikhail 15
Battle
    of Masurian Lake 33
    of Stalingrad 65
    of Tannenberg 33
    of Tsushima 25
    of Vistula 49
Battleship *Potemkin* 27
Bloody Sunday 25–7
Bolotnikov, Ivan 11
Bolsheviks 18, 36–8, 40, 42–7, 49, 50, 55–6, 68
Brezhnev, Leonid 66, 68–9
Bonaparte, Emperor Napoleon 12–13

Catherine the Great, Tsarina of Russia 12
Chernenko, Konstantin 69
Cold War 65–6

Communist Party 55, 62, 66, 68, 70
Concentration camps 60, 63
Constituent Assembly 47
Czechoslovakia, invasion of 68

Decembrists 13
Demonstrations 25–6, 36, 40
Duma 27, 29, 31, 36, 38

Education 45, 52, 62

Fabergé jewellery 28
Farming
    Collective 58–60, 66
    State 58–60
Feudalism 4–5, 9, 14
Five Year Plan 58

Gapon, Father 25–6
Germans 33, 36–7, 63–5
Golden Horde, the 5
Gorbachev, Mikhail 69–70

Herzen, Alexander 14
Housing 9, 21, 29, 50, 53, 60–61, 66
Hungary, uprising in 66

Industry 19–21, 23, 39
Ivan the Terrible 6–7

Kadets 47
Kerensky, Alexander 39–42, 44
Khrushchev Nikita 66–7
Kornilov, General Vladimir 41
Kosygin, Alexi 66, 67, 69
Kronstadt naval station 42, 50
Kulaks 23, 55, 58

Leningrad (St Petersburg and
    Petrograd) 7–8, 13, 25, 27,
    29, 33, 36, 38, 41–44, 64
Lenin, Vladimir Ilyich 16, 18,
    27, 36–7, 39–41, 43–47, 49,
    51–52, 55–6

Marx, Karl 16
Mensheviks 18, 38–9, 42, 47
Mongol Empire 5, 7
Moscow 27, 64

Nicholas II, Tsar 24–5, 27–8,
    35–6, 48
New Economic Policy 51–55

October Manifesto 27
Octobrists 62

Peasants 6, 9–11, 14–15, 23–4,
    27, 34, 39, 45–6, 50
Peter the Great 7–8
Petrograd, see Leningrad
Poverty 9, 23, 28–9, 35–6, 42,
    50–51, 60
Proletariat 16, 21
Provisional Government 36–40

Pugachev, Emilian 11

Railways 20–21
Rasputin, Gregory 30–31, 36
Razin, Stenka 11
Reagan, Ronald 69
Red Guards 44–7, 49
Reforms 14, 16, 33
Religion 4, 45
Revolution 16–19, 23
    July 40
    1905 27
    November 43–46
Romanovs, the 7, 19, 28, 31, 36

St Petersburg, see Leningrad
Salt Talks 69
Satellite states 65–6, 68–9
Show trials 62
Soviets 27, 37–8, 41, 43
Stalin, Joseph 36, 55–8, 60, 62–6
Stolypin, Peter 24
Strikes 25, 27

Tchernishevsky, Nicholas 15–16
Treaty of Brest Litovsk 47
Trotsky, Leon 27, 41–3, 47, 49,
    55–7, 62

War, First World 31–7, 40
War, Russo–Japanese 25, 27
War, Second World 63–5
White Army 46, 49
Winter Palace 25–6, 38, 44
Women's rights 38, 66
Working conditions 22–3, 53